BRICK
BUY BRICK

INVESTING IN HOUSES OF
MULTIPLE OCCUPANCY

Matador
9 Priory Business Park,
Wistow Road, Kibworth Beauchamp,
Leicestershire. LE8 0RX
Tel: (+44) 116 279 2299
Fax: (+44) 116 279 2277
Email: books@troubador.co.uk
Web: www.troubador.co.uk/matador

ISBN 978 1783064 953

British Library Cataloguing in Publication Data.
A catalogue record for this book is available from the British Library.

Typeset by Troubador Publishing Ltd, Leicester, UK
Printed and bound in the UK by TJ International, Padstow, Cornwall

Matador is an imprint of Troubador Publishing Ltd

INTRODUCTION

This book in the Brick Buy Brick educational series has been written in association with Tigrent Learning UK, the UK's most respected provider of professional training programmes.

Tigrent and its associated network of industry experts and partners have a wealth of property investing knowledge. Tigrent trainers and customers derive from all ages and backgrounds and have over a decade's experience of working with new and existing investors from all over the world.

This book in the Brick Buy Brick series looks at Houses of Multiple Occupancy or HMO as an investment strategy and the opportunities it offers to the property investor. It looks at what exactly constitutes an HMO and examines the pros and cons of HMOs compared to other Buy To Let properties. It also explores the obligations of a landlord of an HMO in terms of Health & Safety requirements and licences, gives guidelines for dealing with tenants and also provides hints and tips on how to find the right opportunities for HMOs and how to make a profit.

For more information and to give us any feedback on your reading experience please visit:

www.brick-buy-brick.co.uk.

CHAPTER ONE

HMO & THE PROPERTY INVESTOR

What is an HMO?

HMO stands for 'Houses of Multiple Occupancy'.

In England and Wales, according to the Housing Act 2004, HMOs are defined as 'entire houses or flats let to three or more tenants from two or more households who share a kitchen, bathroom or toilet.'

In Scotland HMOs are defined as houses used as the only or principal residence of three or more qualifying persons from three or more families.

For the purposes of this book, a property is defined

as an HMO if there are three or more people living there, forming two or more households.

A household can consist of either a single person or members of the same family who live together and includes married couples, couples who are living together and people in same-sex relationships.

Landlords of HMOs must meet certain standards and obligations over and above those required for non-HMO rented accommodation.

Houses in multiple occupation, also known as houses of multiple occupancy, are residential properties where 'common areas' exist and are shared by more than one household.

Common areas may be as significant as bathrooms and kitchens, but may also be just stairwells or landings. HMOs may be divided up into self-contained flats, bed-sitting rooms, or lodgings.

HMOs are not the same as purpose-built flat blocks,

since most will have originally existed as large buildings in single household occupation. Legislation also makes a distinction between those buildings occupied mainly on long leases and those where the majority of the occupants are short-term tenants.

The advantages of HMOs for the property investor

Growth market

With the shortage of housing in the UK, communal living is a way for people to find an affordable place to live. Changes to the housing benefit rules mean that single people under 35 years old are now only entitled to a room in a shared house, meaning many more people are seeking accommodation in the HMO market. Difficult financial conditions have led to people seeking more cost-effective solutions to their housing needs. From those on benefits to those with well-paid jobs, lots of people these days are looking for quality shared accommodation.

High money-making potential

The fact is, a carefully chosen and well run HMO property can make the property investor drastically more money than a single let. You don't have to worry about what might happen to the price of property; it's a bonus if the capital value improves but you are already making a good profit every month.

Less hassle

Having a large number of tenants at one location means you don't have to chase round a number of different addresses in order to fix problems and you're not driving across town to do viewings at various different flats.

Less risk

More tenants does not necessarily equate to more risk. After all, one problem tenant is merely one fifth or sixth of your total rent income rather than 100% of the rent in a single let flat.

When you invest in an HMO property you have to know what you're doing and manage it properly or it could cost you. As the landlord, it is your responsibility to make sure your HMO is properly run.

There are serious consequences for getting it wrong but if you follow the legislation and do things right, there are very good opportunities for you.

First of all, it is important to learn that different local authorities throughout the UK have different rules about HMOs and it is essential that you consult with the local authority at every stage of setting up an HMO.

Categories of HMO

There are various terms for HMOs. When people talk about HMOs they might use any of the following terms:

Category A – Bedsits

In practice it depends upon each council what constitutes a bedsit. Some councils will define a

5

bedsit as any room in an HMO that has a lock on the door. Normally a bedsit is a room that is occupied by a tenant for their exclusive use but there is a communal kitchen or bathroom. Each tenant in a bedsit will have their own tenancy agreement. If you provide a communal living space in the property then it is not a bedsit, but you need to ask the council what they think a bedsit is.

Category B – Shared houses

Shared houses are HMOs if there are three or more people forming two or more households. This is quite specific; in the case of two people sharing a property who are not in a relationship and do not form a single household, if one of those people becomes pregnant the arrival of their baby will add a person and thus make the property an HMO.

Category C – Lodgings

When you are also living in the property the definition of an HMO of three or more people forming two or more households doesn't include you. So you can have two lodgers and it still won't be an HMO, but if you have three lodgers it does become an HMO. You do have to physically live in the property to have lodgers, and you may need to check your mortgage agreement to see whether you are allowed to have lodgers.

Category D – Hostels, guest houses, hotels & B&Bs

These are not HMOs. In a hostel or hotel there has to be a change of use. Hostels, guest houses, hotels and B&Bs are classed as C1 accommodation, whereas HMO is classed as C4, even though both HMOs and hotels share some legal requirements, like fire doors. You will need planning permission to turn a former B&B into an HMO and you may encounter difficulty in some cases. Some tourist towns, for example, may want to maintain a certain number of rooms for holiday makers and will turn down your request for planning permission.

Category E – Residential homes

Residential homes will also require permission from a council for a change of use into an HMO. In the case of care homes, these require registration under the Registered Homes Act 1984. There are many types of care homes, e.g. for the care of the elderly or infirm, care of the mentally ill or for those dependent on drugs or alcohol.

Category F – Flats, flatlets and maisonettes

These are flats and studio flats which can share a common main entrance, but are self-contained behind their own 'front door' and do not share amenities.

It is important to note that there is no clear boundary between each of these categories and a house (or even a part of a house) might move between each of these categories over a period of time.

If you have purchased a large property that has been converted into flats (completely self-contained units), but it was converted before 1991, then the pre-1991 building regulations will have been used, and the council will class this as an HMO. This is because the property will not conform to the regulations on fire resistance that were brought in under the 1991 regulations. If there is any doubt, you will need to do a survey to check the details of the conversion.

TOP TIP: Do a pre-planning application before you buy the property. Unlike an official application for planning permission, pre-planning will not go public, so the vendor need not know about it.

Getting successful pre-planning permission doesn't get you official planning permission but it is a way of checking if there are any obvious issues with the planning. Pre-planning permission will make it clear that in general the council can foresee no specific reasons why you can't do what you want to do, even though it in no way constitutes planning permission.

If you have succeeded with pre-planning but the council subsequently encounters a problem and they refuse you official planning you can appeal. One good thing to know is that the appeal doesn't go to the council, it goes to an independent arbitration panel. You can, of course, always apply for full planning before you buy because you don't need the consent of the seller to do this. However, remember that this application will go public and the seller will know what you are planning to do and they might put the price of their property up in response.

CHAPTER TWO

LICENSING

In England and Wales it is an offence, punishable by fines of up to £20,000, to let properties that fall under the mandatory licensing provisions of the Housing Act 2004. Rental properties that need a licence under the Act are HMOs of three or more storeys, with five or more occupants, who form two or more households, and households includes partners and relatives living together, using shared facilities such as a kitchen or bathroom. Lofts and basements are included in the storey count if they are used as living accommodation. In Scotland it is a criminal offence to give permission for a house to be occupied as an HMO without a licence. The maximum penalty is currently £5,000. The application for a licence must be made by the owner, even if the property is leased to or managed by another person or organisation.

As a private landlord of an HMO, the council will expect certain things from you. They will expect the property to meet basic minimum standards, sometimes referred to as the 'Decent Homes Standard', they will expect you to behave in a fair and reasonable way to your tenants and, as stated above, in some cases they will want you to hold certain licences.

Mandatory HMO licensing

You will need a mandatory licence where the property consists of 3 or more storeys AND 5 or more tenants AND 2 or more family groups (including couples) in the property.

A storey doesn't usually count if it's a cellar or loft, unless either is used as a living space or are in a fit state to be used as a living space. You will need to get clarification from the council regarding their definition of a living space. As a rule, however, loft conversions will count if they are in use or have been constructed for use.

Selective HMO licensing

Selective licensing for HMOs are dependent on a designation from the local authority. The Housing Act of 2004 gives local authorities the power to introduce the licensing of privately rented flats or houses within designated areas. The aim of selective licensing is to improve the management or condition of rented properties and address the impact that persistent anti-social behaviour from tenants can have on the area, particularly those areas with low housing demand.

In an area of selective licensing, all private landlords must obtain a licence and if they fail to do so, or fail to achieve the required management standards, the local authority can take enforcement action, for example issuing a fine or in some cases, taking over management control of the property. Selective licensing designation can last for up to five years and can be renewed.

Information required for an HMO licence

The information required for an HMO licence will be whatever is deemed appropriate by the local authority for regulating the management of use of the house, including:

- Personal information about the owner, agent and manager.
- CRB checks/declarations.
- Previous enforcement action – which might show you are not a reputable landlord.
- General information – tenancy agreements, inventories, etc.
- A works plan showing how you aim to convert the property into an HMO.

Information contained on an HMO licence

The licence will contain various conditions to the

holding of the licence including:

- Those pertaining to regulating the use or occupancy, e.g. the occupancy limit.
- Those to prevent anti-social behaviour. Ultimately your sanction is that you can evict the tenants.
- The facilities and equipment to be kept in good order or, where necessary, to have them repaired – being able to check smoke alarms, for instance.
- A requirement to reduce or remove hazards.

Mandatory conditions for an HMO licence

- Gas safety certificates, which must be produced to the local authority.
- Electrical safety certificates.
- Furniture safety declarations – all furniture has to comply with certain standards for fire safety.
- Smoke alarms must be correctly installed and in good working order.

N.B. You will have to make a copy of the HMO licence available to all tenants or licensees.

The Decent Home Standard

A home is considered decent if it is:

Free from category 1 hazards (according to the Housing Health & Safety Rating System) and in reasonable repair (see Chapter Three – Health & Safety).

CHAPTER THREE

HEALTH & SAFETY

Your HMO property will have to be assessed according to the Housing Health and Safety Rating System (HHSRS). This is a risk-based assessment system which the local authority must use when evaluating the safety of your property. It will be carried out after you have applied for an HMO licence, but it also may be carried out as the result of a complaint from a tenant. The assessment system concerns itself with those things that would be normally considered the responsibility of the landlord.

The rating system for hazards is based on the effect of a defect in a property. There are 29 identified hazards (including damp, structural faults, etc). It is assessed against the most vulnerable group that might live in the property, (e.g. the elderly or very young), the likelihood of harm occurring and the effect of harm.

At the end of the assessment a 'hazard rating' will be given. There are four classes which relate to degrees of perceived harm. Category 1 is the most severe rating, regarded as risks that could lead to death, paralysis, severe pneumonia or severe burns. Councils have a duty to act on category 1 hazards and the power to take action on category 2 hazards.

In terms of which hazards are considered the most significant, and where the council will take action, these are:

Excess cold

You can find the full guidelines for what constitutes excess cold and how to take preventative steps against it by doing an internet search for 'CIEH excess cold guidelines'.

Carbon monoxide

Carbon monoxide is odourless and can be a killer. There is no requirement for carbon monoxide detectors in a property but, especially if the boiler is sited in a bedroom, they are highly advisable.

Fire

You are required to provide a minimum of 30 minutes of protection from fire by implementing the fitting of fire doors, the use of fire-proof plasterboard, smoke alarms, and so on (see fire safety).

Radon

This is the second biggest cause of lung cancer in the UK after cigarettes. It is only found in certain areas of the country, specifically where a substrata of rock in the ground gives off radon gas, so you will need to check on a map showing areas affected by radon.

You are required to check up on all the regulations

required for the prevention of these hazards, as well as those relating to food safety (having adequate provision for the preparation and storage of food, i.e. one food cupboard per tenant) and personal hygiene (i.e. the provision of bathrooms, although different councils will have different regulations as to the number of bathrooms required for tenants).

You will also need to consider the issues of crowding and space and the risk of falling on stairs.

Reasonable repair

Key building components (external walls, roof structure and covering, windows and doors) should have reasonably modern facilities and service. You should provide:

- A reasonably modern kitchen (20 years old or less).
- A kitchen with adequate space and layout.
- A reasonably modern bathroom (30 years old or less).

- An appropriately located bathroom and WC.
- Adequate insulation against external noise (where noise is a problem).
- Adequate size and layout of communal areas for blocks of flats.

You should also provide a reasonable degree of thermal comfort, i.e. effective insulation and efficient heating in the property.

Risk assessment

Your property will be assessed for the 29 hazards which will produce a banding and a category. This reflects the judgement of the surveyor, so it's not standard. If a surveyor uses the system fairly the opinions shouldn't vary too wildly between surveyors. It is open to challenge, however, if you feel the judgement is unfair.

The risk assessment is part of a logical sequence. A base-line assessment is carried out based upon the risk to the most vulnerable group. After the base-line assessment, it is who exactly is living in the property that is taken into consideration. If there are no elderly people in the property and there are not likely to be, then this will be taken into account in the report. If there are no children due to live in the property then the local authority is supposed to not be as stringent with, for example, safety around windows.

Fire safety

Local authorities do not normally require fire extinguishers in Buy To Let accommodation. In HMOs, however, the provision of fire extinguishers is required.

Local authorities will also expect you to supply a fire blanket in each room used for cooking. Each local authority will have their own requirements for fire safety, however, so you must check.

Fire extinguishers

Fire extinguishers are required in all HMOs where sprinklers are not fitted.

The types of extinguishers required must suit the environment they are there to protect.

Note that all extinguishers are painted red, but each type of extinguisher will also have a 'colour code' which is a second band of colour upon the body of the extinguisher, which denotes the type of extinguisher it is and what kind of fire it should be used on.

It is reasoned that the correct appliance will be situated beside the appropriate risk.

Types of fire extinguisher

Water – The most commonly used type of fire extinguisher, to be used on fires involving paper, wood, plastic, etc. Not suitable for fires involving liquids or electricity. Colour code: Red.

Dry Powder – Normally found in kitchens. For use on wood, paper, textiles, flammable liquids, flammable gases and electrical fires. This type of extinguisher makes a lot of mess when used because the foam sets hard. Colour code: Black.

Foam – Used for fires involving solids like paper and wood and liquids like oil. Not recommended for electrical fires but they are safer than water if the foam inadvertently comes into contact with electrical appliances. Colour code: Cream.

CO_2 (carbon dioxide) – for use on electrical fires. Not for use on flammable liquids, gas, wood, paper and textiles. This extinguisher needs training to use. Colour code: Black.

Fire blankets – for use on flammable liquids. Requires an extinguisher as a back-up. Best used to protect a person from fire.

Fire extinguisher servicing

All fire extinguishers require annual servicing. Discharge tests are required; with water extinguishers every 5 years, with foam every 5 years, dry powder every 5 years and CO_2 every 10 years plus overhaul.

Beware the internet: Never buy second hand equipment, always buy from a reputable supplier.

Fire safety signs

Being in a fire is extremely disorientating, so exit routes need to be identified and illuminated.

Arrows indicate the direction of travel for escape but there is no arrow on the final exit.

On each turn on a stairwell, you need a sign showing the direction of escape.

An exit sign should never be placed above the kitchen because the kitchen should never be a route of exit.

Emergency lighting

Emergency lighting should come on when the lights go out. They only need to illuminate the route of escape, so are not required in rooms.

Lighting levels need to be uniform throughout the escape route, avoiding different light levels. Lighting should be powered from an independent supply and only areas of power failure need to be illuminated.

Test facilities need to be provided to enable the lighting to be tested without interrupting the supply to the normal lighting for monthly/yearly tests.

Smoke detectors

You need to make sure all alarm sounds are set to the same sound or they will fail the safety check. Alarms must be set to at least 70 decibels at bed-head (a sound detector needs to be placed where you put your head in the bed and it must reach 70 decibels).

In anything over a two storey property you will need smoke alarms classified as LD2 Part 6D, which is a mains interlinked system, i.e. connected to the mains and when one goes off they all go off.

For bedsits & flats (separate self-contained units) you will need alarms classified as LD2 Part 6A, a system with smoke detectors in every room.

Category L systems have automatic fire detection and are intended for the protection of life. They are specified for HMOs that are more than 2 storeys high. These systems must be installed by a qualified technician.

False alarms

Other than in the event of fire, every time an alarm goes off it should be reported as a false alarm. Common reasons for a false alarm include the heat, flames, smoke or fumes from cooking but can include strong winds, radio interference, inadequate servicing, i.e. the presence of dust, dirt or insects, the testing of equipment without notification or malicious operation.

An environmental health officer will need to inspect your property and if they are satisfied with the fire safety provision they will provide you with a certificate proving it meets the required standards.

Other fire safety essentials

Automatically closing fire doors, plus their special liners and seals, must be fitted to all doors within the property.

Safety signs must be fitted on doors. Blue signs consisting of a white asterisk against a blue background should be fixed to all fire doors as a reminder that they should be kept closed, and never propped open.

Fire action notices should be displayed in each flat or bedsit.

Loft hatches have to be fire-protected on the inside. You shouldn't give your tenants access to the roof space.

All visible wiring should be 'fire tough cable' which is coloured red.

Call points, i.e. 'in case of fire break glass', which tend to be 'press here' rather than 'break glass' nowadays to avoid the remote chance of injury. All call points must be of the same type.

Fire Safety Risk Assessment

As the landlord you are required to carry out a fire safety risk assessment on your HMO property. This is something you can download from the internet and fill in yourself. This is how you might go about filling in your fire safety risk assessment form:

Approach the front door. Is the escape route clear as you open the front door?

Can you get out of the property without using a key? You must be able to escape an HMO without using a key. Never have a mortice locking system for the front door of an HMO – have a thumb turn lock instead.

Once inside, into the hallway, lobby or front room, what is there that could be considered a fire hazard?

Is there stuff on the floor, obstacles in the way, papers through the letter boxes, etc?

Mitigating that hazard could be a fire extinguisher or an alarmed smoke detector.

Solution to fire hazard from clutter: Provide storage for trip hazards like coats and shoes, etc.

Kitchen – potential hazards are: the cooker, electrical equipment, presence of an open chip pan, chemicals, overloaded sockets (you should provide two electrical sockets per tenant in an HMO), overflowing rubbish bins.

Mitigation to kitchen hazards: a fire blanket, heat detector, adequate socket provision, rubbish provision and storage for cleaning chemicals.

Bathroom – risks: aerosols, candles around the bath. It is recommended that you ban candles in an HMO full stop! Insist on no naked flames in the property and put this in the tenancy agreement.

The bathroom can be quite a potentially hazardous room for fires. There are no smoke detectors in the bathroom because water vapour can set them off and no fire door is required on a bathroom (unless the boiler is situated there).

When you have completed your fire safety risk assessment, show a copy to all your tenants. It is well worth getting them to sign it to show that they have read it. You can put a copy into your tenants information pack (see Chapter Eight – Managing Tenants).

CHAPTER FOUR

LOCAL AUTHORITIES

As the landlord of an HMO you are required to pay close attention to the various requirements placed upon you by the local authority and these may vary from area to area so you must check on the stipulations each local authority requires for HMOs under their jurisdiction.

Council action in response to hazards

If your property evidences a category 1 hazard, the council are legally obliged to take some kind of action. They will probably take informal action to get you to rectify the situation rather than serving a notice. With a category 2 hazard, the council may consider taking action which might be an Improvement Notice (which can also be suspended until either a date or an event – like when the tenancy changes, for example). The other thing they may do is serve a Prohibition Notice (this can also be suspended), which may say that you can't use part or all of the house or can't use the house for a certain use, i.e. for sleeping purposes.

They can also serve a Hazard Awareness Notice, which does not demand action but everyone including the tenants and the mortgage company will receive a copy of this and it will affect the insurance of the property. In the case of you being sued for injury sustained within the property as a result of the hazard, it will show you were aware of it.

The local authority could choose Emergency Remedial Action where things have to be done straight away, often in the case of electrical faults or anything where there is an immediate danger. In this case the local authority will take action without informing you. You will get notice but only after the event.

Demolition Order – The situation is so bad that it is deemed beyond repair.

Clearance Area – Extremely rare but if there are enough properties next to each other in a state beyond repair then they can all be cleared.

In all the above cases (apart from Hazard Awareness), if you fail to do the works the local authority will do it for you. They will not get the cheapest people to do this, they will charge you for the work and they may in some cases prosecute you as well.

Your defence against council action

Remember that any order or notice can be appealed. You can ask the council how they have arrived at any decision, or you can say that they have not allocated enough time for you to rectify the hazard.

You can say that the notice was served to the wrong

person or it was the incorrect notice. You might say that the assessment was incorrect and that they have made the wrong decision. You could say that the Notice of Entry was not served, that the required works are unreasonable, impractical or that there is a cheaper alternative to the one deemed appropriate by the council.

You could also say that the time period required to do the work is unreasonable. Many local authorities are guilty of coming up with seemingly arbitrary time periods for work, so if you feel there is not enough time to complete the works you can negotiate and get the notice changed to allow a longer time period.

TOP TIP: If you feel hard done by over a safety issue with the local authority you can appeal the decision. You have the right to go to a residential property tribunal, which costs round £150. You might wish to get a solicitor who specialises in environmental health to come along and represent you.

Unless there is an imminent and serious threat to

health or safety as a result of a hazard, you might be served with an informal notice. You will normally get an informal notice first, before you get a formal notice. However, if the local authority does serve a formal notice they may charge you for this, so it's important not to ignore an informal notice.

A Hazard Awareness notice won't go on the Land Registry. It is usually served only to make you aware of a minor hazard but, again, it is important not to ignore this. If one of your tenants hurts themselves in the property they might try and sue you and the fact that a Hazard Awareness notice has been served will greatly substantiate their case.

An Improvement Notice gives you the chance to improve something in the property that is falling below standard.

Being issued with a Suspended Improvement Notice will mean that you won't be able to put another tenant in the property until you've done the required work to rectify the hazard.

A Prohibition Order might stop you letting all or part of the property to certain groups, i.e. the disabled or elderly.

An Emergency Prohibition order may also mean that you can't use certain parts of the property.

The contents of a notice

A notice will be headed with the type of notice it is and who it is served to. It will also give a statement of reasons for the issue of the notice. Schedule 1 of the notice will name the hazards and deficiencies that give rise to them. Schedule 2 will outline the works required to rectify the hazards.

An Improvement Notice must be revoked when it has been complied with. The local authority will make a judgement and in some cases, even if the terms of the notice may not have been complied with in full, they may decide that the work done has reduced the hazard from a category 1 rating and no further action is necessary.

It is possible to appeal against an Improvement Notice, especially if you feel that someone else ought to take action on the hazard or pay the remedial costs. Any appeal must be made within 21 days from the service of the notice.

Non-compliance with a notice may mean incurring a fine from the local authority or they may prohibit you from managing certain types of properties.

Additional local authority powers

In addition to the service of the above notices and orders, local authorities also have the power to issue an overcrowding notice if they feel that too many people are living in the property in relation to the provision of space or facilities. They may issue a Management Order which literally means they can take the property off you. The local authority can issue an Interim Management Order (IMO) which usually runs for twelve months and allows the authority to undertake the remedial works that they require themselves. A Final Management Order can be issued on properties that have been subjected to an IMO, which extends the power to take over the management of the property for a further five years.

A failure to hold a licence for your HMO can lead to the local authority restricting your ability to evict tenants. They can also issue a Rent Repayment Order where they can ask you for the rent that you've collected from your tenants for the period of which you haven't had a licence.

Other notices include those relating to the Public Health Act 1936, The Environmental Protection Act and the Building Act 1984. Under the powers of the Building Act, if your property sustains structural damage the council can keep you and your tenants out of the property until it is safe.

Article 4 Direction

Article 4 Direction prevents or limits the number of HMO properties in an area. It is all about permitted planning. If you live in a conservation area, for example, you are not allowed to do anything to your property without planning, for instance change the windows from wood to upvc.

Generally speaking, if a property is already an HMO it is allowed to remain an HMO.

Residential property is classified as C3, HMO is classified as C4. If you had an HMO (C4) property and turned it into residential (C3) property before Article 4 came in, you can't then turn it back into an HMO.

Article 4 Direction might not be over the whole local authority area, it might only apply to a single part or even a section of streets. Each council will have a date of Article 4 implementation. If you can prove your property was HMO prior to Article 4 implementation, then you are okay, and there are ways you can help prove this was the case. Showing that the property had locks on the door, for example, is a good indication that the property was an HMO. Councils have to publish their Article 4 sites so you can check on a map whether your property falls under Article 4 Direction.

If you can show that the number of HMOs in an area is of low density then you can challenge the council. Known HMOs can be found thanks to a freedom of information request if the council won't inform you. This is public information and the council have to give it to you. Sometimes it will be stored online. Contact the local Environmental Officer for this information and ask how you can obtain it.

As a landlord you may be faced with suspicion from the local authority simply because you are a business and have the aim of making money. It is a sad fact that many local authorities will take umbrage with the fact that you are not a charity. It seems as if their view is that rented accommodation should only be the free provision of the council.

Local authorities need private landlords, however, because they need the provision of property for the people in their area. This is the case with people on housing benefits. Councils may call you up, asking if you have accommodation and they often pay you the rent to house a tenant on benefits.

To be a successful landlord you need to understand what people really want from their relationship with you as a landlord. The tenant and the council want different things.

You need to set up a good relationship with your local authority because they will be able to offer you support when you have problem tenants.

Be suspicious if you have a property in one area and another local authority tries to house someone from their area in your property. This suggests that they are a problem tenant that the local authority has been unable to house.

Benefits claimants

Welfare reforms that came into force in 2013 are changing the way tenants receive benefits.

Under Universal Credit, phased in between October 2013 and October 2017, working-age tenants receive a single monthly payment directly from the Department for Work and Pensions (DWP) and this will include their housing costs.

This is a departure from the situation where many social tenants are used to getting their Housing Benefit paid directly to their landlord.

Pensioners are excluded from Universal Credit and residents of 'exempt' supported housing will have their help with housing costs provided outside of Universal Credit. This means that both these kinds of tenants will be able to continue to have their Housing Benefit paid direct to their landlord.

The government has accepted that there are some working-age people who will not be capable of making a monthly payment, and for these people direct payments to the landlord will also remain.

CHAPTER FIVE

PREPARING YOUR HMO

Preparing your property for HMO

The first thing you need is a works plan showing how you aim to convert the property into an HMO. This is something you have to do as part of your application for an HMO licence for the property. Remember, you only need a mandatory licence for a property with 5 people AND 3 storeys. With fewer people you don't need a licence.

In terms of the conversion, here are a few suggestions.

Decoration

Wallpaper isn't a great idea for decoration in a rented accommodation like an HMO because it is prone to wear and tear and can peel off, especially if the tenants don't ventilate the property adequately. You can allow your tenants to re-paint the property if you wish, and can place certain stipulations on what colours they may use, i.e. neutral, light colours only.

Double glazing

It's better to go to a local double glazing company, rather than a national one, because they will often be better value. In some cases there are even local grants available for this kind of work if your property fits the right criteria. Ask your local authority what grants are available for accredited landlords.

Keys

You need to have a logical key system, preferably

made up of a master, a sub master (for cleaners, etc, which gives access to the communal areas only) and individual keys for tenants. Your own key should let you into all parts of the building. Your tenants should have keys that get them through the front door and into their own room only. These days you have the option of having numeric combination locks on doors, but ask yourself if you think your tenants will always remember the combination, particularly if they are students coming back after a night on the town!

When you come to think about lighting, remember that lighting on all stairs is a required standard.

Project managing a property

Sort out what work has to be done in each room and put this on your works plan.

TOP TIP: Regarding all conversion work in a property, work from the top of the property to the bottom, from dirty to clean. This will minimise mess.

It's a good idea to let out some of the rooms in the property while you are working on the other rooms if you can. You can be getting in rent which can pay the mortgage while you get the rest of the property ready.

If a property is Grade 2 listed, you will need permission to do some renovations, so check the property first before you purchase.

Your carpets should be last things to go in. For an HMO it should be relatively cheap, neutral in colour and hard-wearing.

Laminate flooring is not that advisable for the property, as it can be damaged by high heels and there is also a noise issue, especially for people living below.

Get a quote from your builder and not an estimate, to encourage competition, and add 10% onto this quote just in case.

Make sure all electrical and gas fittings are properly installed and certificated.

Fire doors must be fitted in an HMO (they cost around £200 per door, including the essential liner around the frame).

Bear in mind with conversions that your aim isn't to cram as many people in as possible – which you might be tempted to do to maximise your cash-flow – you're not running a hostel, you are trying to attract good-quality tenants who will want to live in your property.

TOP TIP: If you intend to become the landlord of an HMO, it really helps to get the services of a builder you trust; ideally someone who can help you out of a sticky situation, particularly at weekends when your tenants ring up with a problem which they insist must be fixed straight away.

CHAPTER SIX

COMMERCIAL VS RESIDENTIAL

Commercial valuation & mortgages

For HMO (and Buy To Let), you don't have to have a commercial unit in the property to go for a commercial mortgage. Commercial loans on a commercial business (i.e. shop) are driven by yield, which the bank will make a judgement on.

You might do a commercial loan on the residential part or on all of a purely residential building because a property is in such a bad state no residential lender will touch it, whereas the commercial lender would see the back end value. The commercial loan is driven by an income multiplier and that income estimate is down to the valuer, based on similar rents for similar properties.

Commercial banks, as opposed to high street banks, will also look at the viability and strength of the business and the length of the lease. If your HMO is above a shop, the mortgage might be more expensive, and banks will consider it more of a risk to be above a restaurant or take-away because of the presumed increased fire-risk.

When it comes to a commercial valuation you need to get a commercial broker for a commercial mortgage. It's a specific market with its own rules and regulations. Each property and each business is valued independently. You need to prove demand and you need to prove the figures.

If you go directly to the bank, you have to be very prepared and go with a business plan, but a commercial broker will help you write this. A commercial broker will tend not to charge a fee for their work because they will get a higher procuration

fee from the bank on the loan, perhaps as much as 3%.

The yield

The 'yield' of a property informs you how much annual return you are likely to receive on your investment. It is calculated by expressing a year's worth of rental income as a percentage of how much the property cost.

Therefore, if the estimated weekly rental is £200, the annual rental would be 52 times that, or £10,400. And if the flat cost £100,000 to buy, then the "yield" would be described as 10.4%.

Example of commercial valuation:
3 bed flat above a shop

Market value of the property: £240,000

Rental Income: £2,500 per month (you will need to prove this, and get proof from the vendor of this rental income).

Rental Income per year: £26,000

If the property is really viable it needs to yield less.

The standard yield is 10%.

Yearly income: £300,000

Banks will generally give you 65% of that (loan to value) which equals: £195,000 (this is the actual lending).

Banks do a bricks and mortar valuation, which may be £240,000 and as long as the loan to value is less than this bricks and mortar valuation then they should lend you the £195,000.

N.B. As the landlord, you are responsible for the Council Tax on an HMO. This is different from Buy To Let, where the tenant is responsible for Council Tax. If no-one (or only one person) is in the property you can get a 25% reduction on the Council Tax. You should get one month's grace period (a month off) on this when you take over the property if it is unfurnished.

The lower the yield the banks estimate, the higher the valuation. If you can prove you can get more out of the property in rent, the lower the yield the bank might offer you, perhaps 9% or less.

Commercial finance is very different to residential finance and there are much fewer rules. When you identify a property, investigate both routes (commercial and residential) before you decide what the best one is.

You will normally only be able to get a capital repayment loan with a commercial mortgage, and not an interest-only one.

If you are buying a new property and cannot prove its rental income you will probably need to run the property for a minimum of one year to show the bank that the property can generate this amount, but again you should talk to each lender to see what their particular rules and stipulations are.

Doing a capital AND interest mortgage gives you more control over how you pay back the debt, because you can chunk it down.

Commercial lending is looked at in terms of each particular business case rather than simply the rules that cover residential lending.

The 6 month rule

In commercial property, as opposed to residential property, the 'six month rule' doesn't exist. The six month rule is a restriction on how quickly you can do property deals. It was put in place by the Council of Mortgage Lenders (CML) to curb unscrupulous lending to high-risk people. Basically, it stops the property investor from re-financing a property, unless they are a first-time buyer. It only comes into play if you are using a mortgage product. If you are a cash-buyer it doesn't apply. If you want to sell a property after you've bought and refurbished it, you have to wait six months to show that proper work has been done on it, to guarantee a value increase and to help protect vendors.

CHAPTER SEVEN

FINDING TENANTS

As a landlord you will naturally want the ideal tenant, one who pays their rent on time every month and causes no problems like damage or anti-social behaviour, but you should be aware that you will undoubtedly encounter tenants who fall short of this ideal. You should decide what kind of tenant you want and put your energies into finding the best tenants you can, to reduce the chances of problems further down the line.

So how do you go about finding tenants, and crucially the *right* tenants for your HMO property?

If you see lots of To Let signs in a certain area, it's clearly one where there is a lot of letting potential. Ring up the number on the sign and take the opportunity to look round the property – it pays to check out the competition. Remember, though, that often properties are occupied but they haven't got round to taking the signs down yet.

If you see an example of 'guerrilla marketing' like a home-made sign saying 'I buy houses' you can phone the number and say 'so do I', and ask if they have any properties that they don't know what to do with.

If you're looking to buy student accommodation, ring the local university and ask them for a university accommodation list.

Go to the offices of local lettings agents and lettings management companies, form a relationship and ask them what they know.

Put signs on your properties saying 'Rooms To Let'. They are cheap to make and there are many companies on the internet that will print you a sign.

You can use guerrilla marketing tactics like making home-made signs. You can even use your car to display a sign. Some people go the whole hog and get their entire cars sign-written with their company and telephone number!

The newsagent's window is a tried and tested advertising site. You can also advertise on internet sites like gumtree.com and easyroommate.com.

It's well worth speaking to the human resources departments of large companies. The advantage here is that you can choose the kinds of companies you'd like your ideal tenants to work for. The really big employers will know staff that need accommodation. Employment agencies are also good people to talk to as they may need accommodation for their workers from overseas.

TOP TIP: When thinking about an HMO that might suit nurses, speak to the local hospital to see if they are planning any large purpose-built nurses' accommodation in the area which may stifle your flow of student nurses. The same goes for university students and purpose built halls/student accommodation.

When to advertise

If you have already let your property and it is occupied, then from December to January is a good time for signing up students. With non-students, i.e. 'professionals', you can advertise at any time.

In December, find out whether your current tenants are leaving or staying. Then, in January, advertise for the next academic year.

You can also advertise for students out of season. Ask the university if they have any PHD or ERASMUS students because these won't necessarily start in September.

If your property is empty and hasn't been let to

anyone yet, you need to start advertising immediately to offset your mortgage. You don't have to advertise it as an HMO, you can just say 'room to let' and fill one or two rooms first.

CHAPTER EIGHT

MANAGING TENANTS

Once you have found your potential tenants, how should you manage them?

Tenant's application form

Your potential new tenants should fill in an application form with their details:

Their name and home address.
Their previous address.
Their contact details: mobile/home landline/email
Their National Insurance Number – be aware that some students will not know what this is.

Identification: Photo ID/passport/driving licence. (If they have a non-EU passport, ask if they have permission to stay).

Background information on applicant, including:

References: previous agents/landlords.

Bank details: standing order / guarantors (i.e. parents if students) – you will need to credit check these guarantors.

You can use companies like creditsafe.co.uk, leaseguard.co.uk, homelet.co.uk to do reference checks.

Next of kin.

College ID: ID number/course/tutor

And you will need all this information for every one of your tenants.

Contracts & agreements

With HMOs the length of the tenancy tends to be around 6 months. With students it tends to be 12 months; from July you can charge half rent until September, when the student moves in, and then charge full rent all the way through until the end of the academic year in June.

Whenever you take any money from a tenant give them a receipt or an advice slip.

Extra clauses to tenancy agreements can ban smoking in communal rooms. As stated previously, however, by law you cannot stop a tenant smoking in their room.

Inventory or statement of conditions

It is your responsibility to ensure that the property is ready and clean on time and it is essential that you provide your tenants with a full inventory of the contents of the property, together with a statement of each item's condition.

Be specific when you write an inventory, and where applicable, accompany it with photographs, which you can get signed by the tenants in order to back it up.

Do not make an opinion when it comes to an inventory, state facts; say what you see and only what you see.

Get the inventory signed and dated by your tenants on move-in day, and provide them with hard copies, plus photos if necessary.

You can use an inventory clerk to compile your inventory if you wish.

Welcome packs

Provide your tenants with a welcome pack upon arrival. This might contain:

A welcome note.

Emergency contact details and the numbers for a locksmith and tradespeople.

A copy of the tenancy agreement.

A copy of any notices.

A copy of standing orders.

A copy of any certificates, i.e. gas, electric, HMO, fire alarm and those for the fire extinguishers.

Photocopies of the manuals for the various appliances – copies rather that the originals because these will invariably be lost at some point.

Rent collection

Set up standing orders for rent collection. You have control over a standing order and it can't be cancelled by the tenant like with a direct debit.

Arrears

You should impress upon your tenants the importance of informing you of any potential difficulties they might have with meeting the rent on time. Early communication of possible difficulties will allow you to plan accordingly. You also need to set up a system to deal with potential rent arrears.

A suggested rent arrears system:

After 3 days non-payment of rent – send a text.

After 7 days non payment – send a letter plus a fee (of £5 or £10).

14 days late – 2nd letter plus fee (£10 or £15).

21 days late – call in person to the property in order to collect.

1 month late – issue a Notice to Quit Section 21 (see eviction procedures).

Refusal to pay: Court action. (In the case of guarantors, the guarantors will also have refused to pay).

Maintenance

You have a legal requirement to maintain the property. Make a list of preferred tradespeople that you would like your tenants to use.

Log all maintenance calls and log who made the call.

Contact the tradesperson requesting a time of visit, inform the tenants of the time the tradesperson will call and ask the tradesperson to inform you when the job has been done.

Check in with the tenants to ensure they are happy with the repair.

Tenancy Agreements

Just because you put something in a tenancy agreement, it may not be legally enforceable. You can put 'no pets' but you can't actually stop someone from having a pet as, thanks to the Human Rights Act, it is someone's human right to have an animal companion. The same goes for a 'no smoking' stipulation, which cannot be legally enforced in a private room, only in communal areas or in common parts of the property. If someone declares that they are a smoker you could perhaps ask for a higher deposit to cover future cleaning costs.

It really is a personal decision what goes into your tenancy agreement. One thing you can have is the details of guarantors, which you might want, particularly in student accommodation, as well as details of tenancy deposits. You don't want to overwhelm tenants with an excessively punitive 25 page tenancy agreement; you are looking to welcome people into the property rather than put them off!

To make sure your tenants are abiding by the tenancy agreements you will need to do regular checks, either personally or by getting your management company to do them.

Eviction procedures

Section 21 is what landlords use to evict tenants from their property. It is a piece of legislation which allows you to evict tenants after the fixed term of Assured Shorthold Tenancy (AST) has expired. In practice this means that a minimum of two months notice must be given to tenants before possession of the property is re-taken and this is dated from the time when the tenant receives the notice, not when the notice is posted or written.

A Section 21 notice may be served at any time once deposits have been paid but while you are allowed to give the Section 21 notice at any time during the tenancy period, you can't force your tenant to leave before the fixed term has expired. So you need to make sure that the date at which possession is required is at least a day after the expiry of the fixed term.

If you serve notice during the fixed period, you will need to use a Fixed Term Notice, which comes under section 21(1) b.

After the expiration of the AST fixed term, the tenancy becomes a Periodic Tenancy, unless a further fixed term is agreed upon.

You can use Section 21 throughout the periodic term, but instead of serving a Fixed Term Notice (section 21(1)b) you would serve a Periodic Term Notice, under section 21(4)a.

A Periodic Term Notice must give two months' advance notice and this notice must end on the last day of the tenancy period, with the date of required possession being the day after this.

Tenancy periods are normally defined by how frequently rent is paid. If your tenants pay their rent monthly, then the tenancy period is one month; if they pay rent weekly, then the tenancy period would last one week.

Section 8

A Section 8 notice to quit is an eviction notice used in cases of serious damage to the property or, most commonly, where the tenant has fallen into arrears. Unlike a Section 21, which is simply a letter that you write, a Section 8 comprises of an official form that you have to download from the internet.

As the landlord you are not able to legally evict a tenant without first obtaining an order for possession from the courts. Before you apply for this order you must serve the Section 8 notice to quit on the tenant. This formally states that you intend to seek possession of the property and also the grounds on which possession is sought.

Because any errors contained on the Section 8 notice can delay you gaining possession, it is strongly advisable to get legal advice before issuing a Section 8. You can serve the notice by post or in person and if there is more than one tenant, it must be served on all of the tenants. It is a good idea to have someone witness you serving the notice and to allow three working days from the postal date for the notice to arrive.

If you issue a Section 8 you should always issue a section 21 with it because that should trigger whatever system you have in place for finding a new tenant.

Eviction hints and tips

Don't use signed for or recorded delivery to serve your eviction notices as they can be refused and they won't be deemed served.

If a tenant refuses to go after all notices have been served you will need to initiate court proceedings. You can apply to the courts for an N5B, which can be downloaded and has to be filled in absolutely correctly. The landlord must sign this form, not just the letting agent.

Scotland has different rules for tenant evictions. Eviction notices must be served in person, for instance.

If the tenant leaves their belongings in the property you could issue a notice of abandonment, but this doesn't really work because the tenant can come back and say they didn't abandon them. In the tenancy agreement you should state how long a property can be vacant before the tenancy is deemed surrendered (together with rent arrears) which is usually 28 days.

CHAPTER NINE

CASE STUDY – RICK WALTON

Thirty-seven year old Rick Walton is a successful property investor who also trains other investors and speaks at numerous investment training events. His background is in pharmaceutical engineering, an industry he worked in after graduating from Loughborough University with a first-class engineering degree. Rick says 'While I was at GlaxoSmithKline I was headhunted by Pfizer. At 29 I found myself earning fifty grand a year, but although I had money, I had no assets and nothing to show for it. Plus, I got fed up with the job when I realised I couldn't progress. I had this restless feeling that I wanted something else for myself other than engineering.'

Although motivated by a desire for personal fulfilment, it was a family tragedy that eventually provided the impetus for Rick to begin his property investment career. Rick explains, 'We lost my wife Lucy's mum Elaine to cancer aged just fifty-two and this was a massive turning point for me. My wife was grieving so badly that I knew I wanted to give her support and spend more time alongside her. The loss of Elaine also brought home to me how precious life is and how I didn't want to spend time doing something I didn't enjoy.'

Rick's wife Lucy had begun to invest in property while she was still studying at university. 'I'd seen how successful Lucy had been with property, so I started to investigate and do some property investment courses; in Distressed Property, Buying At Auction, Buy To Let and Creative Finance. I decided that if I wanted to do this properly I needed to know what I was doing, which is why I invested in myself to get educated.'

The first deal Rick did was to purchase a distressed property at auction, which he then used as a Buy To

Let. 'I genuinely couldn't have done this without the training I took because this deal put into practice what I had learned on all four of the courses I had taken.'

Rick describes this first investment deal as a 'fairly straightforward paint and fix job'. He says, 'It was a two-bed flat, which I still have and which makes me £600 a month. My wife Lucy and I built a model based on this; buy a two-bed flat for under £100K, refurbish it for no more than £10K, refinance, pull our money out and go again. It was a real cookie-cutter approach and it worked really well.'

Figuring that he needed around £1,800 per month to achieve financial freedom, Rick achieved that goal within 15 months of his first investment. After successfully investing in six Buy To Let properties, Rick and Lucy then felt confident enough to add an HMO property to their portfolio.

Rick says 'I was glad we made that leap to HMOs because I soon saw how well they worked for us and made us the most money. Because of this, HMOs are what we've stuck with ever since.'

In terms of income Rick says that his HMO properties, which are typically turned into 5-8 bedroom houses, regularly generate over £1000 a month.

Regarding what to look for when it comes to HMOs Rick says, 'Typically we look for houses with large double bedrooms and plenty of communal space that really work for our target professional market.'

More recently, however, Rick has started to focus on the conversion possibilities of former care homes, disused pubs and fading bed and breakfasts which, Rick points out, are unfortunately quite abundant in some parts of Kent.

Rick stresses that more than smaller Buy To Lets, HMOs require very good systems of maintenance and management. 'With larger properties and more tenants living in them than your average home, the wear and tear and general day to day management can be more demanding. But with a good team of people around you, who can put things right quickly and stay on top of the paperwork, HMOs can be very lucrative.'

Rick's property portfolio is based mainly in his home county of Kent because he found that the numbers worked in this area and it allowed him to remain close to Lucy and their children Harry and Amelie.

Rick explains, 'I started investing as a way of creating a new lifestyle, one where I could remove the need to go off to work and instead spend more time with my wife and children. It was also a way of giving myself a pension for the future.'

Asked if he has achieved all his ambitions yet, Rick shakes his head. 'With me, I don't know how to switch off. I have achieved a large pension pot and I no longer need to have a job, but in my mind I've still got more potential to do even better things than I've done so far.'

Rick describes his lifestyle before he began investing

in property as one where he was working long hours, had disposable cash but no assets. 'But now I'm much more in control. I'm busy out of choice and my commute is twenty yards downstairs to my office, so I have far more time to be around my family. The steady income I get from property means I feel more secure and in control of my financial affairs. I don't now worry about how things are going to be paid for or stress about nasty bills.'

Rick's advice for the would-be investor? 'First of all know why you want to get involved in property investment and what you want to achieve. And if you are going to do it, invest in yourself first.'

Rick puts it like this: 'You don't know what you don't know. With property there are so many things you should be aware of if you're going to be successful. No-one is born a property investor; it's something you have to learn. It's not easy because it takes energy, guts and focus but it is simple in the fact that it is straightforward, uncomplicated and with the right education anyone can do it.'

CHAPTER TEN

CASE STUDIES

These case studies show two examples of converting a property into an HMO. They are purely illustrative and are designed to show you how varied HMO property can be and how creative you can be with putting together a deal. When it comes to the figures, there's no right or wrong way to invest in HMOs as long as it is profitable to you, but these case studies show you what you need to be thinking about when it comes to HMO property.

Case study one: B&B to HMO

Ex-B&Bs can make excellent HMO properties. Here

is one example, setting out how a property investor might approach turning a B&B into a successful HMO.

There is a ten-bed B&B up for sale. It is situated on a junction, close to the station and town centre. It is being advertised as a commercial property and has six parking spaces that come with it. It has four storeys, including the basement and there are three bedrooms on each storey, plus a communal room and a living area for the family who run it. There are three bathrooms throughout the property in addition to six ensuites attached to rooms. Every room is also equipped with a hand basin.

The main benefits to the property investor with B&Bs like this one are that a lot of the work normally associated with turning a residential property into an HMO has already been done for you, especially in relation to the various plumbing issues because you've already got pipes leading to the sinks in the rooms, some ensuite facilities, plus a lot of the doors will be fire doors, etc.

Let's now have a look at the finances.

You have a potential for 12 rooms in the HMO, if you include the communal room and the family's living area. Let us say that you rent out these 12 rooms at £75 p/w. Over a year this would bring you £46,800 in rent (or £3,900 rent p/m)

The property is on the market for £350,000.

The couple who currently run it as a B&B are getting £50,000 a year, but in order to run it as a B&B they have to cook breakfasts every morning, clean the rooms, and so on, which they no longer want to do.

You the property investor might put in a cheeky offer of £275,000, despite the owners saying they want £320,000. You can then start to negotiate, but your aim is to get them to settle for around £300,000.

In this case you might also look to set up a Purchase Option and move them onto an Option contract where you give them a down payment now and complete the purchase in 6 months time (See Brick Buy Brick – Lease Options).

During this time you could get the owners to be interim managers of the property while you set about getting it up and running as an HMO, and you can give them a payment of £2000 p/m for doing this (not bad for them, considering the B&B is only making them £50,000 a year anyway).

So it would cost you £14,000 to get into this deal. This is made up of: £12,000 (6 months of £2,000) + Council Tax of £1,000 which you offer to pay + £1,000 solicitor's fees for setting up the Option Agreement.

So you have to find £14K plus an estimated £25K for the refurbishment.

The value on the property on the back end (after the refurbishment) is £400,000 which means the bank should lend you more money on it, potentially 70% loan to value, which is £280,000.

N.B. You should get the refurbishment done before you get a revaluation.

The beauty of this scenario is that if the purchase price you settle on after negotiation is £300,000, then the deal becomes almost self-financing.

Case study two: A 3 bed residential property to 5 bed HMO

A much more straightforward HMO conversion, and one you are perhaps more likely to contemplate as a property investor just starting out with HMO is converting a normal family residence into an HMO.

There is a 3 bedroom residential semi-detached house that you wish to convert into a 5 bed HMO, based on using the living and dining room to create two extra rooms.

Property asking price: £150,000

What would it earn you in rent?

5 beds @ £80 p/w = £1,733 pcm (5 x 80 x 52 weeks divided by 12 months)

The deal:

Purchase price: £115,000
Obtain a 75% Loan To Value Mortgage @ 6% = £86,250

Which leaves £28,750 required in deposit.

Your outlay:
£431 per calendar month in loan.
£260 – 15% of the rent for your management company fee.
£347 – 20% of the rent for MOE (Monthly Operating Expenses like Council Tax, gas, electricity, TV licence, broadband, etc.)

Total outlay pcm: £1,038
Total income pcm: £1,733 (in rent) minus £1,038 = £695

Refurbishment costs:

£3,000 (smoke alarm and emergency lighting)

£2,500 (all furniture inc. white goods)

£500 (property valuation for mortgage purposes)

£2000 (fire safety fittings)

£500 (licence fee)

£500 (redecoration)

£1000 (legals: searches and surveys)

Total refurbishment costs: £10,000

Cash required on purchase (refurb + deposit): £10,000 + £28,750 = £38,750

You get a loan of £38,750 on 8%. Monthly, that is £258 p/m (which has to come out of your cash flow).

£695 minus £258

= £437 cash-flow coming in per month.

CHAPTER ELEVEN

CONCLUSION

This introduction to HMO is designed to help the investor understand the potential benefits of this investment strategy. The key here is understanding all the legal requirements that are needed with HMOs, like exactly what constitutes an HMO, the licensing involved and all the health & safety regulations which are required. Knowledge is power and arming yourself with the right knowledge is crucial for success. A successful property investor should see HMO property as an important category in the Buy To Let market. We wish you the very best of luck on your Brick Buy Brick journey.

This book is part of the Brick Buy Brick series, created in association with Tigrent Learning Ltd, who have been at the forefront of UK investment training since 2002.

www.brick-buy-brick.co.uk

NOTES

NOTES

NOTES

NOTES

NOTES